WOMEN'S STORIES *from* HISTORY

STORIES OF WOMEN IN THE
1960s
Fighting for Freedom

Cath Senker

raintree
a Capstone company — publishers for children

Raintree is an imprint of Capstone Global Library Limited, a company incorporated in England and Wales having its registered office at 7 Pilgrim Street, London, EC4V 6LB – Registered company number: 6695582

www.raintree.co.uk
myorders@raintree.co.uk

Edited by Penny West
Designed by Philippa Jenkins
Original illustrations © Capstone Global Library Ltd 2015
Illustrated by Franco Rivoli - Advocate Art
Picture research by Tracy Cummins
Production by Helen McCreath
Originated by Capstone Global Library Ltd
Printed and bound in China by Leo Paper Group

ISBN 978 1 406 28949 7
18 17 16 15 14
10 9 8 7 6 5 4 3 2 1

British Library Cataloguing in Publication Data
A full catalogue record for this book is available from the British Library.

Acknowledgements
The author would like to acknowledge the following main sources for this book:
Betty Friedan: Her Life, Judith Hennessee (Viking, 1999); *The Feminine Mystique*, Betty Friedan (Penguin, 2010); *Fighting All the Way*, Barbara Castle (Macmillan, 1993); *Life So Far: A Memoir*, Betty Friedan (Simon & Schuster, 2000); *Mary Quant Autobiography*, Mary Quant (Headline Publishing Group, 2012); *Barbara Castle: Politics & Power*, Lisa Martineau (André Deutsch, 2000).

We would like to thank the following for permission to reproduce photographs and artwork: Capstone: Advocate Art/Franco Rivoli, 6, 12, 25, 30, 40, 49, 56, 64, 69, 78, 95, 97; Corbis: Hulton-Deutsch Collection, 100; Getty Images: Spencer Grant, Cover; SuperStock: ClassicStock.com, 4.

Contents

Introduction

By 1960, American and British women felt like second-class citizens. Growing numbers were going to university, but they usually ended up in inferior jobs to men. They were paid less and found it hard to advance in their career. Women were frequently secretaries or teachers, but they rarely managed companies or became head teachers.

In the USA, African American women were treated even worse because of racism. They tended to do low-paid, backbreaking, exhausting jobs. Even though they had the right to vote, African American people in southern states faced discrimination when they tried to exercise this right. For example, voters had to be able to read and write, and many African Americans could not.

Frustrated with their situation, in the 1960s, American and British women began a movement for equal rights and freedom. This book tells the stories of four of those women.

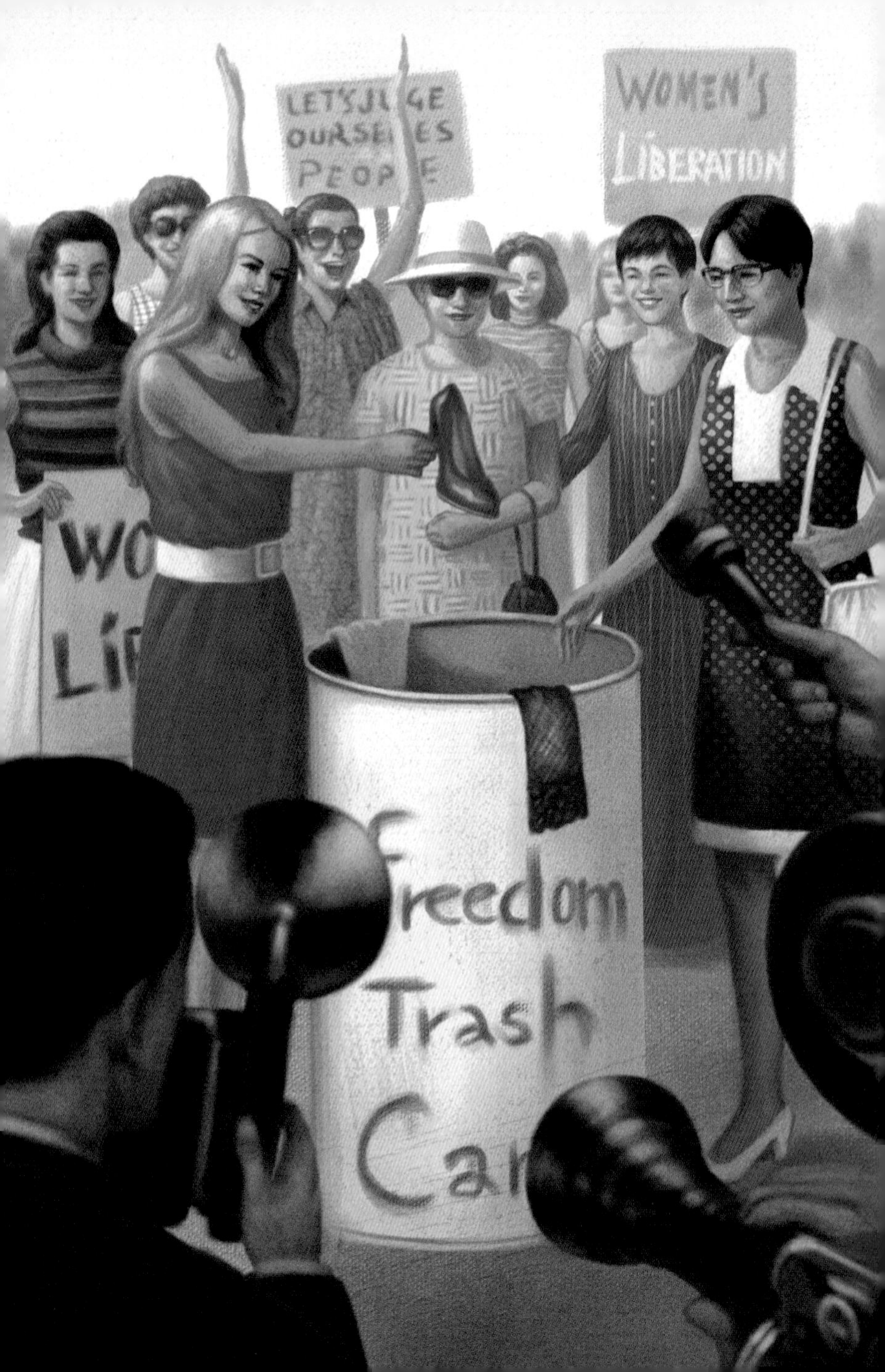

WOMEN'S LIBERATION
Freedom Trash Can

Betty Friedan:
Founder of the US women's movement

In the years after World War II (1939–1945), as the US economy boomed, many Americans moved to comfortable homes in the suburbs to raise their families. Adverts, television and films quickly began to support an ideal of a "perfect" suburban life held together by the glue of a perfect housewife. For women, this caused some problems. In giving their total focus to homemaking duties and perfection, these women had little room for pursuing their own interests or careers.

A woman named Betty Friedan helped change the way Americans viewed the role of women. In 1963, she published an influential book called *The Feminine Mystique*.

In it, she wrote:

> Each suburban wife struggles with it alone.
> As she made the beds, shopped for groceries,
> matched slipcover material, ate peanut butter
> sandwiches with her children, chauffeured Cub
> Scouts and Brownies, lay beside her husband at
> night — she was afraid to ask even of herself the
> silent question — "Is this all?"

Throughout the book, she argued that many women felt unfulfilled in this role of housewife and needed other outlets for their talents and energy. As a result of this book, more and more Americans – and, eventually, people around the world – re-examined the role of women at home and in the workforce. Some people agreed with her, while others felt offended or challenged by her ideas. Yet, over time, her work changed the lives of millions of women.

Betty Goldstein (born Bettye, but she dropped the "e" from her name) was born in 1921 in Peoria, Illinois. It was one year after American women finally achieved the vote, following a long campaign by the women's movement. The eldest of three children, Betty had a younger sister, Amye, and a brother, Harry Junior. As a child, Betty was not comfortable with who she was. She wore glasses, had poor coordination and suffered from asthma.

Betty got on well with her father, Harry. But her relationship with her mother, Miriam, was difficult. Miriam was an intelligent, talented woman who had edited the women's section of the local newspaper. After she was married and had a family, however, she gave up her job, as was expected at the time.

Years later, Betty said:

> When people, reporters, historians, [ask] why
> me, why did I start the women's movement,
> I can't point to any major episodes of sexual
> discrimination in my early life. But I was so
> aware of the crime, the shame that there was no
> use of my mother's ability and energy.

Looking back, Betty believed that much of the tension in her household was partly the result of her mother feeling frustrated and unfulfilled in her role as a housewife.

Betty was highly intelligent. After school, she attended Smith College, where she graduated with a degree in psychology. However, when Betty was offered the chance to study for a PhD, she decided against it. She had noticed several female academics who were single with no children. Betty was scared that pursuing a career would leave her lonely and unhappy. In this way,

Betty was feeling the tensions she would later explore in her work. She already firmly believed in the equality of women. But she also knew that she wanted to marry – although she would not accept a husband who thought women belonged at home.

In 1944, Betty moved to Greenwich Village, New York, and took a job as assistant news editor at Federated Press, a small newspaper agency. Two years later, she moved to UE News. That year, she met Carl Friedan, who ran a small theatre company. Carl and Betty married the following year, and although they loved each other, their relationship was stormy.

Their first son, Daniel, was born in 1948. In those days, most women gave up work to have a family. But Betty returned to the office when Danny was less than a year old. She stayed at UE News until she became pregnant again and lost her job. At the time, it was normal to fire pregnant women if they did not volunteer to leave.

After the birth of her second son, Jonathan, in 1952, Betty began a freelance writing career, penning articles for women's magazines. It was easier to combine with raising children than an office job. Four years later, she gave birth to her daughter, Emily.

In the 1950s, there was little childcare for small children, and women were still expected to do all the housework. Carl was a good father, spending plenty of time with the children, but Betty ran the home single-handedly while balancing this with her freelance writing.

The Friedans frequently moved house, but wherever they lived, Betty was always busy organizing in the community. In Rockland County, she invited academics to visit at the weekends to talk to the local schoolchildren about their subjects and help to broaden their minds. This gave her some fulfilment. Although she had a working life as well as a family, she was beginning to sense that many women who were purely housewives were not fulfilled in their role.

When she attended her Smith College 15-year class reunion, Betty had the perfect chance to test out her theory. She prepared a questionnaire for her classmates. She asked how their lives had changed since graduation and if they were happy. Most of these highly educated women were now housewives. In fact, it was extremely common at the time for women to marry straight out of college and have children. There was even a debate in the media about whether higher education was wasted on women. Betty decided to write a book based on her findings. It took her five years to write and *The Feminine Mystique* was published in 1963.

By this time, the situation for women was changing. The movement for African American civil rights was growing, and women were heavily involved in this. Increasing numbers of women were going out to work. One-third of women had jobs, and one-third of married women were working. Yet many educated women were working in jobs that did not use their full potential. They were asking themselves "Is this all?" Within society, people were debating: should women only be housewives?

In *The Feminine Mystique*, Betty explained how women were told that their main function in life was to be a wife and mother. If they failed to adjust to this role, they would lose their femininity and not be seen as "proper" women – a terrible fate.

With her background in psychology, Betty drew on the theory of psychologist Abraham Maslow. He found that once people had met their basic needs for food, shelter and clothing, they needed some kind of purpose in life to achieve their potential. Betty showed that housewives were being denied their chance for human growth. They felt belittled, restricted to the role of homemaker caring for their husband and family, with no independent interests.

She wrote:

> The only way for a woman, as for a man, to find herself, to know herself as a person, is by creative work of her own.

The Feminine Mystique received mixed reviews. Some women hated it because they felt Betty made their lives as homemakers appear worthless. Later, in the 1970s, others criticized her for only talking about the situation of white, middle-class women. The book did not reflect the lives of working-class or most African American women. But for many women, it was groundbreaking. Betty later recalled:

> It was quite fantastic the effect [the book] had, it was like I put into words what a lot of women had been feeling and thinking, that they were freaks and they were the only ones.

And I called my first chapter "The Problem That Had No Name". And, I mean, I still meet women all these years later and they say, "You changed my life or it changed my life," meaning the book.

Betty's ideas did indeed encourage some housewives to change their lives. One day, Betty's son Jonathan went to visit his neighbour, Peter. He asked Peter's mother, "Where are the cookies?" But she had returned to university to do a social-work degree. "I'm working," she replied. "Tell your mother we're all working now, more power to her."

The title rapidly became a bestseller, as women nationwide rushed into bookshops seeking it out. Betty went on radio and TV talk shows and gave lectures around the USA to promote it. She was even invited to the White House to speak to President Lyndon B. Johnson about the issues she had raised.

The Feminine Mystique changed Betty's life. Now she was well known, earned good money and enjoyed a comfortable home life. Her children were getting older and more independent, and she had a maid to cook the meals.

Other women were also clearly beginning to change their lives for themselves, but they faced an uphill battle. They were barred from many jobs and had to bear the cost of childcare while they were working. The idea arose for an organization similar to the African Americans' National Association for the Advancement of Colored People (NAACP) to fight for women's rights. In *The Feminine Mystique*, Betty had argued that cultural attitudes towards women needed to change in order for women to realize their full potential. A women's organization would be a platform to achieve this change.

Excited by the idea, in 1966, Betty met with

civil-service professional Catherine East and a Justice Department lawyer, Mary Eastwood, to discuss setting up such an organization. They then met with other women who agreed to become involved. Betty came up with a name for this new women's movement – the National Organization for Women (NOW). Betty and other leaders invited powerful women to join. African American lawyer Pauli Murray was a founding member, but most were white, middle-class women.

NOW decided to campaign on equal rights at work. It would oppose sex-segregated job advertisements, which divided posts into men's and women's jobs. The group would push the government to set up childcare centres and improve the rights of women in the workplace.

NOW's membership quadrupled to 1,200 in the first year. During 1967, Betty and other members of NOW campaigned for a change in US law through the Equal Rights Amendment (ERA), which would give women equal rights at work. (While the ERA came close to existing, it was never made law.) NOW also fought for the right to abortion, to give women more control over their bodies and when they had children.

Younger, more radical women soon started to flock to NOW. These women were passionate about a struggle for women's liberation: freedom from domination by men. However, other NOW members, including Betty, felt the pressing need was for women's rights within existing society. Betty once said:

> Some people think I'm saying, "Women of the world unite — you have nothing to lose but your men." It's not true. You have nothing to lose but your vacuum cleaners.

These different opinions led to huge debates within the movement.

Despite the changing membership of NOW, Betty remained its national leader. She travelled around the USA and to Europe to lecture and exchange views with other women's organizations.

During this period, Betty experienced serious personal difficulties. She separated from Carl and they agreed to divorce. She firmly believed in women's right to end an unhappy marriage, but personally found it an exceedingly hard decision to make. Betty feared facing life alone.

Over time, some members of NOW sought to challenge society's expectations of women to look feminine for the pleasure of men. Betty disagreed with the opposition to femininity and took pride in her personal appearance.

Younger members of NOW also supported

publicity stunts to gain attention. At first, Betty also disliked this approach. But she changed her mind after a major protest against beauty pageants.

Every year at the Miss America contest in Atlantic City, pretty young women paraded in bathing suits, hoping to be awarded the Miss America title. Many women in NOW believed it turned women into objects for men to gaze at and judge on their looks alone. NOW decided to organize a surprise event at Atlantic City.

Gathered on the streets outside the Miss America contest, NOW women crowned a live sheep as their Miss America, comparing the beauty contest to livestock competitions held at county fairs. They hurled uncomfortable items that they felt forced to wear into a Freedom Trash Can: girdles (tight garments to pull in the stomach), false eyelashes and high-heeled shoes.

The nation's media recorded the event. One report exaggerated wildly, saying that women had thrown their bras into the bin and set fire to it. This never happened, but the myth of "bra burning" by feminists was born.

Betty had conflicting feelings about this event. She did not like the radical, "bra-burning" stereotype of feminists that was spread in Atlantic City. But, at the same time, she realized that publicity stunts brought widespread publicity to the cause.

In 1969, Betty and NOW organized Public Accommodations Week to highlight discrimination against women in public places. In February, Betty and other NOW activists walked into the Oak Room bar at the Plaza Hotel in New York, which did not allow women. After Betty and other women sat down, not only did the waiters refuse to serve them, but they even removed the table! Betty, dressed elegantly in a fur coat and dark sunglasses, calmly said to reporters: "It looks like we are not going to be served" and then left. The event and image received widespread media attention.

Keen to bring together the different strands of the women's movement, Betty organized a Congress to Unite Women. More than 500 women attended. They passed several resolutions, including the demand for free 24-hour childcare centres and the passage of the ERA.

By 1970, NOW had expanded to 100 chapters (branches) and 3,000 members. Betty realized that her time at the head of NOW was coming to an end. She had already been president for four years and her opinions were increasingly different from the younger, more radical members. New women leaders were on the rise within NOW, such as Gloria Steinem and Bella Abzug.

At the 1970 board meeting of NOW in Chicago, Betty announced she would be giving up the leadership. As her parting move, she wanted to plan "something big, something so big it will make national headlines".

She proposed a women's strike on the 50th anniversary of women gaining the vote, called the Women's Strike for Equality. Betty later changed the proposed strike to a march.

On 26 August, Betty led a crowd of 50,000 women down Fifth Avenue, New York, during the rush hour.

They filled the streets, holding homemade banners with slogans such as "Don't cook dinner! Starve a rat today!" At the rally, speakers called for abortion on demand, free 24-hour childcare centres, and equal opportunities in jobs and education. Betty's speech received the loudest cheers. She said:

The women who are doing menial chores in the offices as secretaries put the covers on their typewriters and close their notebooks and the telephone operators unplug their switchboards, the waitresses stop waiting, cleaning women stop cleaning and everyone who is doing a job for which a man would be paid more stop... And when it begins to get dark, instead of cooking dinner ... we will assemble and we will carry candles alight in every city to converge the visible power of women at city hall.

Women in other cities also marched in this national outpouring of women's demands. It was one of the best days of Betty's political life.

Although no longer the leader of NOW, Betty continued to work for women's rights. She directed her efforts towards bringing more women into politics. In July 1971, she and Bella Abzug co-founded the National Women's Political Caucus (NWPC). It campaigned to encourage the political parties to include more women representatives, so that women could "make policy, not coffee".

During the 1970s, Betty fell out with younger leaders of the women's movement, particularly Gloria Steinem and Bella Abzug. She criticized them harshly in her newspaper and magazine articles and distanced herself from the radical image of younger feminism. Still, she retained a large following within the movement.

Betty turned to academic work too. She bitterly regretted not studying for a PhD, which would have enabled her to take up a university post. Yet she did receive visiting professorships in universities, where she discussed women's role in society.

Still in demand as a speaker, she organized and attended conferences and seminars, and was active in the international feminist movement. She also wrote more books, although they did not have the impact of *The Feminine Mystique*.

Betty mellowed with age and she staged reconciliations with people she had fought with in the past. She kept up a lively social life, holding lots of parties and befriending younger women who could update her about the latest ideas in the women's movement. At the end of her life, she was happy, independent and wealthy. Betty Friedan had written an enormously influential book, founded the largest US women's organization of the 1960s and helped to make women's rights an international issue. Without her, young women today would not have many of the opportunities that they take for granted.

Ella Baker:
Struggling for civil rights

In the long struggle to gain civil rights for African Americans, many leaders are remembered for giving powerful speeches. Equally important was the behind-the-scenes work of a woman called Ella Baker. For decades, Ella worked tirelessly as she organized grassroots efforts to achieve civil rights. A modest person, she was not interested in being in the spotlight. Rather, Ella wanted to help ordinary people join the cause and become leaders themselves, saying:

> The major job was getting people to understand that they had something within their power that they could use.

Ella also believed strongly in educating young people so that they could understand the issues at stake and take up the cause in the future. She was widely respected for her ability to relate to – and listen to – the concerns of young people. For this reason, she is remembered by the nickname "Fundi", a Swahili word for a person who passes on knowledge to the next generation.

Like most African Americans born in Virginia in the early 1900s, Ella was the grandchild of slaves. Before slavery ended in 1865, her grandparents had endured life as the property of white masters. By the time Ella was born in 1903, her family was doing reasonably well. Her father was a waiter on a ferry, so he was away working most of the time. When he was around, he made sure Ella and her brother and sister had fun. For example, if the circus was in town, he took them.

Ella's mother, Anna, had given up school

teaching to raise the family. She taught her children to read before they started school. Anna always helped poor people, sharing food with them and tending the sick. She was active in the church and brought the children to its gatherings. Ella joined the church when she was just nine and developed excellent public speaking skills at the meetings.

Ella's family moved to Littleton, North Carolina, where she finished school. She was a bright student, but there was no further education available for African American people in her town. So she headed to Shaw University in Raleigh, North Carolina.

At university, Ella became involved in political issues and developed her sense of fairness. For example, she fought for the right of male and female students to walk across campus together, setting an example of activism for other women. In her senior year, the president of the university wanted to expel her for being a troublemaker. But she was a talented student – she would later graduate at the top of her class – so her teachers defended her!

Female African American college graduates usually became teachers, but Ella did not choose this path because "this was the thing that everybody figures you could do".

Instead, she moved to Harlem, New York, and took a job as a waitress. It was an exciting time to live in this neighbourhood. Young people were enjoying novel forms of African American music and dancing, and discussing new ideas as part of a movement known as the Harlem Renaissance. Ella said:

New York was the hotbed of – let's call it radical thinking.

It was common to stroll along the street and chat, and Ella would talk to everyone she met.

In 1929, Ella briefly found a job writing for *American West Indian News* and *Negro National News*, using her articles to discuss the situation of African Americans. Then, on 29 October 1929, the Great Depression hit, and unemployment in Harlem rocketed.

Ella became executive director of the Young Negroes' Cooperative League. As a cooperative, it was owned and run by the people involved, with the profits shared between them. Ella believed that economic power was a key part of civil rights. She said:

> People cannot be free until there is enough work in this land to give everybody a job.

Ella was involved in other campaigns during the 1930s, including one to encourage the New York City Public Library to employ African Americans. It was successful, and she took a job there herself. Ella fervently believed in developing grassroots leaders in communities – ordinary people who would work to improve their own area. She felt that "strong people don't need strong leaders", meaning the strength of people working together was the most effective tool of all.

In 1940, Ella married Bob Robinson. They never had children, but they took in Ella's niece Jackie because her sister was unable to care for her. Marriage did not stop Ella's political activities. She became Assistant Field Secretary for the National Association for the Advancement of Colored People (NAACP), the main organization fighting for African Americans' civil rights. She was later promoted to Director of Branches.

Ella believed that the NAACP should be as democratic as possible. Often, it sent people into a new area to recruit members. Once they had joined and were paying a subscription, the recruiters moved on. Ella was keen for local groups to do more than pay membership fees. She worked to actively involve the local members in the organization. Ella then encouraged NAACP branches to focus on an important local issue. She argued:

> Take that one thing — getting a new school building; registering people to vote; getting bus transportation — take that one thing and work on it and get it done.

Ella went on tour herself to increase funds and membership of the NAACP. A petite woman, she always arrived beautifully dressed in a suit and neat blouse. She was good at relating to people of all ages and backgrounds, and got on especially well with children. At meetings, she would sit next to quiet people and ask their opinion. She would then raise that person's hand and say, "Here's someone with something to say."

In 1946, Ella resigned from her NAACP job. Despite her efforts, she felt it still focused too much on building the membership simply to raise money, rather than to build a mass organization. Yet, she still helped the organization. In the late 1940s and 1950s, she continued to travel around the country to talk to branches. She urged African Americans to support the NAACP in its campaign for employment laws that were fair to African American people, for better health conditions and "against every measure, proposal and practice designed to oppress the underprivileged".

A major cause for Ella was the campaign to register African American people to vote. Because some US states required a literacy test in order to vote, she helped adults learn to read and write.

In 1957, Ella faced a new challenge as she helped to set up the Southern Christian Leadership Conference (SCLC), a civil rights organization headed by Martin Luther King Jr. She was one of the few women leaders of the civil rights movement, although many women were involved. She noted after the launch meeting of SCLC:

> At this meeting there were over 100 men present. I don't think that there were any women there except me.

The following year, she moved to Atlanta, Georgia, to work on voter registration. She held discussions with Martin Luther King Jr on how to develop the movement. Ella hoped the SCLC would create a mass movement of people all over the USA taking action on civil rights, rather than simply promote Martin Luther King Jr to fight on their behalf.

Ella had a difficult year in 1959. First, she split up with her husband. She also left SCLC over differences in opinion about how the movement should develop and her frustration with the SCLC leaders. They were male ministers who were not used to having their views challenged, and she felt they did not listen to her. But a significant new struggle was on the horizon.

In February 1960, four African American students sat down at a Woolworth's lunch counter in Greensboro, North Carolina, causing gasps of shock all around them.

The lunch counter was for white people only. The staff refused to serve the students because of the colour of their skin, but they refused to leave.

These courageous students were protesting against segregated public facilities in the South, where it was legal to offer separate lunch counters, libraries, parks and swimming pools for black and white people. The facilities for African Americans were always inferior to those for whites.

Over the new few weeks, these "sit-in" protests spread like wildfire around North Carolina and other southern states. They met with angry reactions. White men shouted abuse at the students, attacked them with eggs or itching powder and jostled or shoved them.

Ella was greatly excited by the enthusiasm of the student activists. She invited the sit-in leaders to a big gathering in April 1960, called the Southwide Youth Leadership Conference, to discuss the way forward.

More than 200 students packed into Ella's meeting. A heated debate arose over whether students should be part of SCLC or set up their own organization. In the end, they established their own group, the Student Non-Violent Coordinating Committee (SNCC).

At this gathering, Ella gave an important speech that summarized her long-held beliefs about the power of people working together. She told the audience:

> The [conference] made it crystal clear that current sit-ins and other demonstrations are concerned with something much bigger than a hamburger or even a giant-sized Coke.

Whatever may be the difference in approach to their goal, the Negro and white students, North and South, are seeking to rid America of the scourge of racial segregation and discrimination — not only at lunch counters, but in every aspect of life...

Here is an opportunity for adult and youth to work together and provide genuine leadership — the development of the individual to his highest potential for the benefit of the group.

Ella believed that the new generation held the key to change. She felt that the students should be able to act independently, even if it meant they made mistakes. One sit-in leader, John Lewis, commented that although Ella was older than they were, "in terms of ideas and philosophy and commitment she was one of the youngest persons in the movement".

The students greatly respected Ella for the way she operated. She had a quiet and intelligent way of leading. Unlike many other adults, she did not try to tell the students what to do. In large meetings, she listened to what everyone had to say. Sometimes she asked useful questions to focus the discussion. Then she would express what she felt most people were thinking, and usually they agreed she was right. SNCC worker Judy Richardson recalled:

> You never felt that she had a personal agenda that she was trying to put on. It was always about what is good for the organization, for black people, for whatever the larger issue was.

Ella did not aim to achieve fame as a leader; she always encouraged people to work out their own solutions.

By helping to form SNCC, which became one of the most important movements of the decade, Ella made a significant contribution to the struggle for civil rights.

The lunch-counter sit-ins were SNCC's first major success. Within a few months, the counters were desegregated, including the Greensboro Woolworth's lunch counter. The courage of the activists eventually helped to achieve the Civil Rights Act of 1964, which made the segregation of public facilities illegal.

In 1961, a major argument arose in SNCC. Should the movement focus on voter registration? Or should it focus on direct action like the Freedom Rides, when groups of black and white people boarded public buses travelling to the southern states and asked to be served in bus terminals along the route? Activists argued loudly on both sides, but Ella easily solved the problem. The movement could do both. Direct action against segregation could continue and so could the campaign for voter registration, which was still greatly needed.

Ella travelled around the southern states to offer her support to SNCC activists, who were often attacked for their efforts to encourage voter registration. For example, in October 1962, SNCC's newspaper *Student Voice* reported that three SNCC workers were shot and wounded. Ella recognized the tremendous bravery required to participate in the movement.

Another crucial leadership role for Ella was organizing education and training to support SNCC's activities. Ella realized that the students required an understanding of the broader issues as well as practical advice to ensure their survival out in the field. She arranged training workshops and helped to develop new leaders.

Always happy to go where she was most needed, Ella moved to New York in 1963 to focus on fundraising for the civil rights movement. She was the main organizer of a Carnegie Hall benefit concert on 1 February, the third anniversary of the first sit-ins. The star-studded cast of musicians included The Herbie Mann Sextet and Thelonious Monk. At the event, all the SNCC workers present gathered on stage to loud applause. The benefit raised a tremendous $8,000 (£4,800), worth around $60,000 (£36,000) today!

During the same year, Ella started work for the Southern Conference Educational Fund (SCEF), which aimed to challenge the racist attitudes of many southern whites and help to foster integration. For example, SCEF hired white student Robert Zellner to visit white campuses and attempt to change students' views. Ella felt at home in SCEF, believing that it was genuinely concerned with improving the lives of ordinary people.

The work fitted with her principles of working for equal rights for men and women, both black and white. As she explained in a speech to a large meeting in Hattiesburg, Mississippi, in 1964:

> I was never working for an organization; I have always tried to work for a cause... All of us are guilty at this moment for having waited so long to lend ourselves to a fight for the freedom, not of Negroes, not of the Negroes of Mississippi, but for the freedom of the American spirit, for the freedom of the human spirit.

In the same year, Ella took part in the ambitious Mississippi Freedom Summer programme. Mississippi had major racial inequality. Only 7 per cent of people registered to vote were African American, the lowest percentage in the country, and schools for African Americans were very poor quality.

Knowing the risk of violent opposition, thousands of civil rights activists travelled to Mississippi to help make a change by registering voters and educating children.

SNCC's work continued after the Freedom Summer and, as ever, arguments frequently arose over organization and tactics. A dispute broke out over the structure of SNCC – should it be loose and flexible or tight, with strict rules? It grew so fierce that some students started fighting.

Ella said nothing but started singing "We shall overcome", one of the theme tunes of the civil rights movement. Everyone joined in and soon the atmosphere returned to calm. Ella had proved once again her ability to bring people together.

Despite the difficulties within SNCC, the voter registration campaign now paid off. In 1965, the Voting Rights Act was passed. It outlawed restrictions on voting such as literacy tests, and spurred voter registration. SNCC celebrated victory in one of its major struggles.

Ella always had her eyes on the next challenge. She understood that the struggle for political rights was linked to economic issues. African Americans were generally confined to the lowest-paid jobs, and black women worked in the lowest-paid jobs of all. They suffered more than white people from unemployment, poor housing and poverty. Urban protests over these issues had forced the civil rights movement to consider economic problems. To this end, the Poor People's Corporation formed to provide loans to businesses run as cooperatives. Ella was delighted with this development, as it built upon her early goals of helping African Americans gain control of their destinies through economic power.

The next stage was more controversial. In the mid-1960s, the radical Black Power movement arose. In cities across the USA, young African Americans declared that they needed to organize separately from white people, to show their independence and growing power. Although Ella believed in her heart that African American and white people should unite and work together, she accepted this new development. As usual, she maintained that young people should be allowed to make their own decisions. To her, this was simply a stage in the movement that would not last forever.

In line with Black Power ideals, SNCC fired its remaining white staff. Naturally, they were devastated. Ella tactfully explained to experienced white activists in SNCC, such as her colleague Virginia Durr, why African American people felt they had to stand on their own two feet.

As the Black Power movement grew, the government became concerned that SNCC was becoming a militant revolutionary organization. The FBI monitored Ella for 20 years, but she was never considered dangerous because she always focused on peaceful change. The FBI reported that:

> The subject is not being recommended for the Security Index [list of people deemed a risk to US security] because in her speeches she has not advocated violence or revolution.

By the 1970s, Ella, now in her seventies, continued to fight for equal rights. She took up the case of prison reform. A far higher percentage of African Americans were sent to prison than white people. Many African American people argued that the police and courts targeted their young men because of racism, and were more likely to arrest and charge them than white people.

In 1971, the Coalition of Concerned Black Americans was formed to focus on how African Americans were treated by the criminal justice system. As ever, Ella encouraged the organization to be democratic and listen to the opinions of everyone.

Although she never wanted to be in the limelight, Ella was publicly honoured late in life. A birthday celebration was held on her 75th birthday, and in 1981, a film was made of her life. Ella will always be remembered as a woman of the grassroots who showed that African American women were capable of leading the movement for social change. She encouraged ordinary black and white people to work together democratically in their fight for the right to vote, to be educated, and to have equal facilities and opportunities. She left as a legacy her special quality of fresh thinking. As Vincent Harding, who worked with Ella in the 1960s, commented:

> If anybody has taught us how to be flexible and change and recreate our ideas and thoughts as time has gone on, Ella Baker has done that.

Barbara Castle:
The most powerful woman in the UK

Barbara Castle rose to prominence in politics at a time when women were not expected to hold powerful positions in government. Using her intelligence and drive, she created her own path and opened the door for women in politics in the future. Her goal was "to inch people towards a more civilized society".

To this end, throughout her career, she supported a wide range of legislation aimed at improving the lives of everyday people and spoke for those who did not always have a voice in mainstream politics.

Born Barbara Betts in Chesterfield, Northern England, Barbara was fascinated by politics from a young age. Outspoken and confident, in 1929, at age 19, she campaigned door to door for the Labour Party. That year was the first election in which all women could vote.

Barbara did brilliantly at school and went on to attend St Hugh's College, Oxford, at a time when few women attended the prestigious university – the first of many barriers to women she would try to knock down. During World War II, she worked as the housing correspondent for the national newspaper, the *Daily Mirror*. Towards the end of the war, she married fellow journalist Ted Castle.

When the war ended in 1945, Barbara decided to stand as a candidate to become a Member of Parliament (MP). That year, the British public did not vote for the Conservative Party of Winston Churchill, who had led the country through the years of conflict. Instead it voted in a Labour government, with a huge majority. Barbara Castle was elected as the Labour MP for Blackburn, and her political career began in earnest.

The Labour government had 21 women MPs – a record number – but they represented just 3 per cent of the total number of MPs in Parliament. Only three of them had important jobs in government. As a female MP, it was expected that Barbara would stick to women's issues, but she wanted to be involved in broader political causes. For example, she had a great interest in African affairs and she believed that Britain's colonies should become independent. With her strong opinions and self-confidence, Barbara soon became a prominent MP.

Barbara had been an MP for nearly two decades when, in 1964, Labour once again won the general election. On a Saturday morning, two days later, Prime Minister Harold Wilson summoned Barbara to his office at Number 10 Downing Street. She was in her cottage in Buckinghamshire, in her dressing gown! She dressed quickly and Ted drove her to London. She recalled:

> My main feeling as I walked through that famous door at Number 10 was one of exhilaration.

Harold Wilson appointed Barbara the Minister for Overseas Development (ODM) because she was knowledgeable about African affairs and popular among African politicians for supporting their independence movements. She was only the fourth woman ever in the UK to become a Cabinet member. At the Guildhall Banquet, a ceremonial occasion to mark the start of the new government, the official announcer proclaimed, "Her Majesty's Minister of Overseas Development and Mrs Castle" – he assumed that Ted was the minister.

Barbara revelled in being an important woman

and the only one in Cabinet. An attractive woman known for her red hair, she adored fashionable clothes and make-up, and always looked glamorous for the photographers. Although she was operating in a man's world, it was important to Barbara to maintain her femininity. At the same time, she once said:

> I have never consciously exploited the fact that I am a woman. I wouldn't dare try that even if I knew how to. I have too much respect for my male colleagues to think they would be particularly impressed.

Behind the scenes, Barbara worked gruelling 16-hour days and slept little. At home, she still did the housework and always cooked Ted's dinner. It was expected of women in those days.

Determined to be heard and to get her way, Barbara tended to speak for a long time in Cabinet, and other ministers found her hard to work with.

However, she proved an excellent manager of her department and won the respect of her civil servants (government department workers).

This was no easy feat. In the 1960s, civil servants were not used to working for a woman. Barbara's permanent secretary (senior civil servant) was Sir Andrew Cohen. He was extremely shy when introduced to her. She recalled:

> No doubt he was embarrassed at having to deal with a woman minister: his wife Helen, a delightful person, told me many months later that Andrew used to swear that he would never work for a woman.

Yet the pair developed a good working relationship.

In Cabinet, Barbara took a lead in opposing the whites-only governments of Rhodesia (now Zimbabwe) and South Africa, arguing for democratic rule by the African majority of the population. However, the UK had business links with these countries so it was hard to push for drastic change while maintaining those connections. Barbara reluctantly agreed to honour an agreement to supply 16 Buccaneer aircraft to South Africa, but only if the UK government rejected South Africa's request for a further 16 aircraft.

As Minister of Overseas Development, Barbara rolled up her sleeves and set about organizing the UK's aid programme to help poor countries. However, Barbara found that her schemes were generally unpopular in the UK. Overseas aid was not seen as a priority, and she had to cope with racism from people who opposed her "wasting" money on poor African countries.

Just as politicians do today, Barbara cleverly found herself a "spin doctor". Journalist Chris

Hall accompanied her on visits to Africa to promote a positive view of her work. On a trip to Tanzania, he staged a photo of her cuddling an African baby to publicize the fact that British aid had paid for the settlement of 100 African families in a model village.

Through publicity like this, Barbara raised the profile of overseas development in the UK. She also achieved real change. In June 1965, Barbara announced to the House of Commons that in future, the poorest developing countries would receive loans interest-free. They had to pay back the loan but without an extra fee. She had persuaded the Treasury (the department that controls public money) that it would not lose any money because the poorest countries could not pay interest on their debt anyway.

Barbara enjoyed working as the ODM but was nevertheless pleased when Harold Wilson promoted her to the Ministry of Transport in 1965.

The transport ministry was an extremely male environment. Barbara was the first female minister; when she arrived, there wasn't even a ladies' toilet she could use. In addition, Barbara was criticized because she could not drive a car. How could she possibly understand the needs of the motorist? Yet she and Ted owned a car, so she felt this was rather unfair.

Barbara understood the challenge of transport.

The number of private cars had risen dramatically from 2 million in 1947 to 8 million, and was forecast to increase to 18 million by 1975. The Ministry of Transport was dominated by highway engineers who were keen to expand the road network. Yet the growing number of vehicles created traffic and environmental problems.

Also, Barbara wanted to support public transport and achieve a balance between road and rail. She faced a struggle to protect the railways. Chairman of British Railways Dr Richard Beeching had written a report that argued for drastically reducing the rail network. She found Dr Beeching tough to argue against, and realized:

> I was in a man's world all right, and I had to impose my will on it.

She reached an agreement that reduced the railway network considerably less than Beeching originally intended.

Barbara also negotiated a plan to encourage the transport of goods by rail to cut down the number of lorries on the roads. She set up a system for goods to be collected in containers at assembly points and carried on high-speed trains.

The safety of travel was another key issue for Barbara. At that time, it was acceptable to drink alcohol and drive a car, which frequently led to terrible accidents. In 1965, 8,000 people died in road crashes. Barbara made it illegal to drink and drive. Police could stop drivers who had committed a road offence, such as going through a red traffic light. They could make them take a breathalyser test to detect if they had been drinking alcohol. The penalty for offenders was tough – they would be banned from driving for a year.

The breathalyser was hugely controversial, and Barbara received many nasty, abusive letters on the subject. Motorists did not appreciate changing their habits, and country pub owners lost money, especially at weekends. One angry motorist wrote, "We'll get you yet, you old cow!"

Not all were so negative. One woman wrote to Barbara:

> Thank you for giving my husband back to me. He used to leave me at home when he went to the pub, now he takes me with him to drive him home.

Despite the unpopularity of the breathalyser, after one year, road deaths had decreased by an impressive 1,200. This was partly because people drove more carefully to avoid committing an offence that would allow the police to breathalyse them.

Another safety issue was seat belts. In other countries, it had been shown that wearing seat belts reduced the seriousness of accidents and saved lives.

But few cars in the UK were fitted with them. Barbara made sure seat belts were included in new cars and inserted into older cars. As with any change, she met with resistance. Some people said seat belts made driving uncomfortable. It was left to future governments to make it compulsory to wear a seat belt – it eventually became law in 1983.

Speed on the roads presented a great danger too. In 1965, a 70 miles (113 kilometres) per hour speed limit had been introduced on motorways as a temporary measure. Two years later, Barbara confirmed that it would be permanent.

Overall, Barbara Castle changed the culture of motoring. It was no longer acceptable to drive extremely fast or to drink and drive. Her work had a lasting impact on road safety. Throughout her time working in transportation, she had to use her determined personality to push through unpopular laws – as she once said, "In politics, guts is all". This did not always make her popular, but she had many important achievements to show for it.

Barbara had done brilliantly well at the Ministry of Transport. In April 1968, she was promoted again, this time to First Secretary of State for Health and Social Security, and Secretary of State for Employment and Productivity. Now in her third Cabinet role, she had achieved more than any other woman in UK politics so far.

Her first challenge came in June, when women workers at the Ford car factory in Dagenham, London went on strike for higher pay. They did a skilled job, machine sewing the upholstery for car interiors. The women argued that they should be paid the same as men for similar work. Their strike threatened to shut down car production at Ford, so the company appealed to the government to settle the dispute.

Barbara invited the strike leaders to come and have tea in her office. The women were angry and would not return to work empty-handed. Ford's personnel officer revealed privately to Barbara that at Dagenham, women received 85 per cent of the men's rate; at other Ford factories, they earned 92 per cent. Ford offered to close the gap. The women received a pay rise and returned to work victorious.

This compromise made Barbara determined to

tackle the issue of equal pay. She wanted women to get a fair deal by making it illegal to pay different rates. But this would take time.

In 1969, in contrast to her success over the Ford workers' strike, Barbara produced a White Paper (a report explaining government plans) that proved disastrous. "In Place of Strife" was an attempt to give rights to trade unions but also to introduce rules to make it harder for workers to go on strike. It included the right to join a trade union and protection against unfair dismissal. On the other hand, the government would have the power to stop "wildcat" strikes – when workers simply walked off the job without a vote to take action. Trade unions and individual members could be fined for disobeying the rules.

Barbara was unable to secure the agreement of the trade unions for this measure, and many Labour Party members turned against the policy.

All she managed was to persuade the Trades Union Congress (TUC) to give a "solemn and binding undertaking" to do its best to stop wildcat strikes.

After this dismal failure, Barbara decided to work for equal pay for women. Pressure for equal pay was growing in society, including among trade unions. Barbara pushed the government to introduce a law, and eventually the Equal Pay Act passed in 1970 – just before the general election.

The Conservatives won the election, and Barbara joined the Shadow Cabinet (the Cabinet of the main party opposing the government). When Labour returned to government in 1974, Barbara became Secretary of State for Social Services. She was still in the media spotlight because female faces remained rare in government – although Shirley Williams now joined her in the Cabinet. Now in her sixties, she found work more tiring but still worked as hard as ever.

Within ten days of achieving office, Barbara announced major changes to the welfare system. She declared that family allowances from the government were not enough to keep wage earners with children out of poverty. Society had changed with the rise of single-parent families. Many mothers were low paid, so their families were poor. Also, pensions had fallen in value, because the cost of living had risen but pensions had not. Barbara promised to increase benefits and pensions.

Barbara introduced child benefit, which was to be paid directly to the mother. Every mother with children at home would get it, so there would be no embarrassment about receiving welfare payments. Also, it was cheaper to offer child benefit to everyone than to attempt to work out who needed it most.

To improve living standards for the poorest elderly people, Barbara introduced a guaranteed minimum pension, which helped those who had no pension through their job. She changed the law, so that when incomes rose, pensions would rise too.

Barbara was determined to make pensions fairer for women. Women generally did not receive an equal pension to men because they tended to take a few years off from paid work while they were raising children. Under Barbara's new pension scheme, working women would pay the same contributions as men and receive equal benefits, even though they retired five years earlier at 60. She explained:

> I knew this was discrimination in their favour, but I argued that men had been discriminating against women for centuries and it would not do them any harm to wait until we could afford to bring down the retirement age to sixty for them as well.

The scheme also improved the situation for widows, one of the largest groups in poverty.

Although she made notable achievements in her post at Social Services, in 1976, Barbara met with a shock. When Harold Wilson retired, the new prime minister, James Callaghan, sacked her. He claimed she was too old to serve, even though she was just two years older than him.

Was Barbara disappointed that she never became prime minister? She clearly was, but she understood why:

> People sometimes ask me if I would have liked to become prime minister. The answer is yes ... [but] in my day the Labour Party was not ready for a woman leader.

Yet just three years later, the Conservative Margaret Thatcher became the first woman prime minister of the UK. Barbara had blazed the trail for another powerful woman to reach the top job in politics.

In 1979, after the defeat of the Labour government, Barbara left Parliament and was elected to the European parliament. That year, her husband Ted died. The couple had been devoted to each other, and she was devastated. Yet she continued in politics, serving in the European parliament for a decade and joining the House of Lords in 1990.

During her long and successful career, Barbara Castle made a significant impact on women's rights, introducing child benefit, equal pay and equal pensions, and acting as a superb role model for female politicians.

Mary Quant:
Fighting for fashion freedom

In the 1960s, Mary Quant changed the way women dressed. She was unique both for her creative vision and for the level of success she achieved during a period when men dominated business. Throughout her career, Mary followed her own set of rules and created new possibilities for modern women.

From an early age, Mary was fascinated with fashion. At her dance class, she saw a tap dancer:

> What struck me was how the whole outfit focused on what she had on her feet: a pair of white ankle socks, and a pair of patent tap shoes with ankle straps.

The young Mary had her first inspiration for the style ideas that would make her famous.

After school in Blackheath, London, Mary attended Goldsmiths art college. She found 1950s London rather dull, saying:

Young people had nowhere to go to keep warm except the cinema, and nothing to do.

Rationing was still in force, and people needed coupons to buy clothes. She found British fashion boring. Mary visited Paris and found it far more exciting.

Yet at London art colleges, students were challenging existing ideas and making discoveries for themselves: new ideas, art, music, theatre and food. Mary herself discovered fellow student Alexander Plunket Greene – APG, as she quickly nicknamed him. It was his extraordinary clothes that she noticed. He was wearing his mother's gold silk pyjama top with hipster (low-rise) drainpipe jeans! It was love at first sight.

After college, Mary began an apprenticeship (training) with a milliner, training to make top-quality hats. In her spare time, she started to make her own clothes. She was influenced by dance outfits she remembered from her childhood and by the beatniks (people who wore alternative fashions, mostly wearing black with berets and scarves).

APG was from a wealthy background, and when he turned 21 in 1955 he inherited £5,000 ($8,400) – worth more than £111,000 (about $170,000) today. With the money, Mary opened a clothes boutique called Bazaar in the King's Road, Chelsea. An excellent cook, APG opened a restaurant below her shop, where the latest jazz music played in the background. The couple's timing was perfect – fashion and music were becoming hugely popular among London's young people.

In the 1950s, men ran the fashion industry. It was unusual for a woman to set up a business, but Mary was determined to succeed. She was enthusiastic about shaking up the fashion world. In the mid-1950s, she felt "fashion wasn't designed for young people". Fashion came from couturiers in Paris, while mass manufacturers churned out cheap copies for ordinary people. But high fashion, such as Dior's New Look, with its long skirts and lavish use of fabric, was impractical for daily life. Mary wanted women to feel free in their clothes.

I wanted to make clothes that you could move in, skirts you could run and dance in.

Mary created clothes for young people that were not available anywhere else, using simple shapes and strong colours. She created unusual combinations, for example masculine suiting fabrics mixed with floaty, feminine ones such as chiffon, satin crepe and georgette.

Mary Quant did not invent the mini-skirt, but she popularized this garment. Women also loved her Peter Pan collar, a little plastic collar with a press stud in the centre, worn to liven up a plain jumper. Mary sold stockings in bright colours to match her knitwear, and long cardigans and shirts that could be worn as dresses. She sold clothes that she and her young friends liked to wear: tunic dresses, knickerbockers (knee-length trousers) and hipster pants.

Mary encouraged young women to be themselves rather than images of their mothers. She wanted them to enjoy their clothes and to dress for their own pleasure, not just to attract men. By doing so, young women showed their independence.

To create her new designs, Mary bought fabrics and accessories from the top-quality department store Harrods. She chopped up patterns to achieve the right sizing, bought sewing machines and started making her clothes.

Mary's innovations stretched beyond the garments to the entire business. Bazaar was an extraordinary shop, with eye-catching window displays – Mary had her mannequins specially constructed to achieve the image she desired. She used unique shopping bags with giant lettering to act as adverts to other shoppers in Chelsea. To ensure her young target market could afford her creations, she charged relatively low prices compared to haute couture (business of making fashionable and expensive clothes for women).

The novelty of the shop did not go down well with everyone. City gentlemen hammered on the windows with their umbrellas shouting "immoral" and "disgusting" when they saw tiny mini-skirts in the windows. But the customers loved the displays.

Bazaar achieved rapid success, and in 1957, Mary opened another store in Knightsbridge, opposite Harrods, designed by up-and-coming designer Terence Conran. That year, Mary married APG and they moved to a flat in Chelsea, close to the first Bazaar boutique. They were a popular couple and frequently entertained visitors with lively parties. TV crews would even turn up to capture the London scene.

The business was expanding, so Mary employed machinists to sew for her. When it grew even bigger, she approached garment manufacturers to produce her designs. Mary found she had to stand up to businessmen to insist that they did what she wanted. They were not used to taking orders from a designer, and especially not from a very young woman.

The Bazaar shops and the King's Road became

the centre of fashionable London. Actors, writers, musicians and models all came to Bazaar. Playwright John Osborne was spotted there, and celebrated French actress Brigitte Bardot. Later, in the 1960s, photographer David Bailey visited, as did model Twiggy and the world-famous Beatles.

Mary helped to revolutionize hairstyles as well as clothing after she discovered hairdresser Vidal Sassoon. He lopped off her ponytail and created the five-point bob haircut that became one of her trademarks. Having short hair freed women from sitting for hours with their hair in rollers to style it. The easy-to-care-for look was ideal for busy women. Best of all, the Vidal Sassoon bob went perfectly with Mary Quant clothes.

It was extremely rare for a woman to be so prominent and successful at the time. Yet she was criticized by the established French couturiers, who thought her designs were vulgar.

Later, she realized that:

"new" is often described as "vulgar" by people who are frightened of change. I had demonstrated that from now on fashion was going to be mass-produced, that the future did not lie in the laboriously hand-sewn designs that were the hallmark of couture.

Mary was ushering in a new era of affordable fashion and paving the way for other female fashion designers.

In 1962, Mary had the opportunity to spread her fashion principles to the USA when she made a licensing agreement with a major US retailer, JCPenney, for clothing and underwear design. Under the agreement, JCPenney bought Mary's designs to mass-produce them in America. Mary designed dresses, sportswear, nightwear, hosiery and underwear. She organized a novel promotional tour in the USA. Until then, fashion shows had depicted middle-aged women wearing corsets (tight underwear) under their clothing and sporting beehive haircuts. In Mary's shows, young models danced wildly to the latest music to promote the garments in an appealing way.

On the production side, Mary persuaded JCPenney to urge its manufacturers to make tights to go with the short skirts and dresses; they were more practical than stockings. Both in the UK and the USA, she inspired the development of the market for tights. She also requested bras that did not distort a woman's natural shape, to achieve the "No-Bra" effect. Mary wanted women to feel comfortable in their bodies and their clothes and not be constricted by uncomfortable underwear.

Looking back, Mary realized the secret of her success with these innovations, saying:

You are more likely to get a design right if you are typical of the market you are designing for, plus I had the great advantage of being female. I could try things out myself.

Mary was constantly on the lookout for new design ideas. When the new plastic material PVC appeared, she designed her Wet Collection (1963), which included tunics, trench coats and smocks.

Mary was also looking for new markets. The same year, she established the Ginger Group, a wholesale business – selling goods in large quantities to retailers to sell on to customers. This lower-priced line was designed to appeal to a wider market than Bazaar and was sold internationally. The range included skinny-ribbed sweaters to wear with tunic dresses and mini-skirts.

With her sure instinct for colour, Mary picked shades that were unfashionable at the time, including mustard yellow, hot ginger and black.

She had fabrics made specially in the colours and designs she selected. By now, she had gained great respect as a businesswoman, and textile manufacturers were happy to follow her orders. Mary Quant was a global brand.

Both the Wet Collection and the Ginger Group proved extremely popular, winning Mary the Sunday Times International Fashion Award in 1964.

Mary aimed to design a head-to-toe look, and her next target was the cosmetics industry. Make-up was expensive and never changed with the fashions. Mary used to do her own make-up with crayons so she could use a variety of colours. For her cosmetics range, she wanted to use fashion colours so women's fingernails could match their dress rather than just their lipstick, as was the norm. She thought women could have fun with make-up, to please themselves rather than men.

In 1966, Mary Quant Cosmetics was launched.

Mary's cosmetics kit included novel colours and textures, with brushes and sponge applicators for applying the make-up. The kit came in an attractive box, convenient to carry in a handbag. The packaging was stylishly designed so women would be proud to flaunt it in public. Indeed, Mary Quant lipstick became the symbol of the new career woman. As usual, practicality was vital. Mary invented waterproof mascara so women could swim or walk in the rain, and their make-up would not run.

Mary revolutionized the sale and marketing of make-up too. Instead of using middle-aged saleswomen behind counters, Mary Quant make-up was sold by young women in mini-skirts and young men in jeans. APG invented fun names for the products: Starkers foundation, Blush Baby blusher, Jeepers Peepers eye shadow and Bring Back the Lash mascara. Mary took a daring approach to adverts, with huge, blown-up faces on billboards. Mary Quant shook up the cosmetics industry.

Mary's natural next step was to create perfumes, and she again broke with tradition. Perfume production was based in Paris, France, where vast factories produced perfumes for the French fashion houses. The business was dominated by men. In 1966, Mary Quant launched fresh fragrances to suit the young women who bought her clothes and make-up.

By now, Mary had achieved great fame and recognition for her contribution to the fashion industry. The same year her cosmetics line was launched, she went to Italy to receive the Piavla D'Ora Award, and was mobbed by adoring fans chanting "Ave Maria" (Hail Mary). She was overwhelmed and realized how lucky she was. To others in this situation, she advised: "Enjoy the fame and never forget your good fortune".

Mary received the OBE (a British award for special achievement) from Queen Elizabeth for the mini-skirt. It was the first time British fashion had achieved such an honour, and it was a woman who had accomplished it. That year, she told her story in her autobiography, *Quant by Mary*.

The awards stacked up: in 1967, Mary was selected as Fellow of the Society of Industrial Artists and won a design award. Two years later, she was chosen as Royal Designer for Industry and added to the British Fashion Council Hall of Fame for her contribution to British fashion. By 1969, it was estimated that up to 7 million women owned a Quant garment.

With the excitement of the 1960s behind her, from 1970, Mary Quant branched out to become an international businesswoman with interests beyond clothing and cosmetics. It was extraordinarily rare for a woman to head a multinational company. She entered interior and textile design, designing soft furnishings for giant British manufacturing company ICI, such as covers for duvets, armchairs and sofas. Mary introduced the idea that you could buy the same fashion colours and patterns for your home as for your wardrobe.

Mary's personal life also changed in 1970 with the birth of her son Orlando. Unusually for the time, Mary did not stop work. Instead she hired a nanny, who travelled around the world with the family.

Clearly, as a wealthy businesswoman, Mary had more freedom than most women. Yet she believed, as a matter of principle, that both partners in a marriage should be able to continue careers when they had children. Her views were radical at the time. She said:

Both need to be able to look after the child and both need their own room to work in alone... Both need to pay for things roughly equally.

When Mary Quant cosmetics started selling in Japan, Mary visited Japan for the first time, bringing APG and baby Orlando. She enjoyed designing for the Japanese market, and the Japanese people loved her designs and make-up.

In the 1970s, Mary Quant's contribution not only to fashion but also more broadly to popular culture was recognized. A special exhibition at London Museum celebrated "Mary Quant's London", and the BBC broadcast a programme about her life.

During the 1980s, the business continued to grow. Mary had the chance to design the interior of her favourite car, the Mini. In fact, she had originally named her skirt after this vehicle. The seats were covered in striking black and white striped fabric.

The decade finished on a low point, however. Doctors told Mary's beloved APG that he would not live for more than two years. This was a huge shock for the family and a difficult time for Mary.

The 1990s brought more awards, and although in her sixties, she continued to play a role in public life. She was approached to be an advisor with the department store House of Fraser. As a fashion designer who had helped to transform the fashion industry of the 1960s, her business knowledge was greatly welcomed.

Looking back at the 1960s, Mary says that she did not set out to shock or upset people – she simply wanted to create lively fashion:

> The sixties mini was the most self-indulgent, optimistic "look at me, isn't life wonderful" fashion ever devised.

She challenged the established cosmetics and perfume industries, producing make-up and fragrances for the women who wore Mary Quant.

Mary had to trust her instincts in the face of powerful men and stand firm. As a woman, she found it particularly hard dealing with manufacturers, who "are not usually the most forward-thinking and respectful when it comes to women's equal rights".

She discovered that fashion is a particularly tough business for a woman with children because it requires ongoing commitment and long working hours. Yet being female turned out to be an advantage for Mary. Post-war fashion was dominated by male couturiers in Paris, but she designed for young women like herself – and she knew what they liked. The fashion revolution of the late 1950s and 1960s changed the industry forever. The mass production of a vast range of garments made fashion widely accessible, providing what Mary called a new "fashion freedom". Mary Quant's role in transforming fashion made her an icon of the 1960s. Other female fashion designers, such as Barbara Hulanicki and Vivienne Westwood, followed in the path that she bravely charted before them. Mary's tremendous impact on popular culture is still recognized today.

Women in 1970

By 1970, there had been major advances for women. In the USA, the Civil Rights Act legally ended racial discrimination. There were no more legal barriers to stop African Americans from voting.

The women's movement achieved crucial steps towards greater equality for women. New rules stopped people working for the government from discriminating against women at work.

In the UK, the government passed an act for equal pay. Another act made it legal to have an abortion in early pregnancy. This gave women more control over when they had children. As in the USA, more women entered the workplace, and some set up their own businesses. Women's rights were firmly on the agenda.

Other important figures

Fanny Lou Hamer (1917–1977)

Fanny Lou Hamer was a prominent civil rights activist from Mississippi, USA. When she volunteered with SNCC in 1962 to help register African American voters in the South, she was fired from her job. Employed by SNCC as a field secretary, she registered to vote in 1963, then taught others how to pass the literacy test so they too could vote. Fanny helped to organize the 1964 Freedom Summer and was a founding member of the MFDP.

Pauli Murray (1910–1985)

Pauli Murray was a lawyer and a leader of NOW. She strongly believed that women needed an organization like the NAACP to fight for their rights. In 1966, she and Dorothy Kenyon successfully argued the case for women to have the equal right to sit on juries.

Shirley Williams (1930–)

Shirley Williams was elected a Labour MP in 1964. She rose quickly through the ranks, achieving junior ministerial appointments in the Labour governments of 1964–1970. She joined the Cabinet in 1974.

Barbara Hulanicki (1936–)

Entering the fashion world shortly after Mary Quant, Barbara Hulanicki opened her Biba boutique in 1964. Hugely popular with young women, Biba sold thousands of mini-dresses in deep colours. The shop became a hangout for artists, rock stars and film celebrities and evolved into a huge department store that survived until 1976.

Timeline

1920 US women are given the vote.

1928 All UK women are able to vote.

1955 Mary Quant opens Bazaar, a boutique in the King's Road, London.

1957 Mary Quant opens a second Bazaar boutique in Knightsbridge, London.

Ella Baker helps to set up the Southern Christian Leadership Conference (SCLC), led by Martin Luther King Jr.

1960 **February**: A sit-in begins at the whites-only counter at Woolworth's in Greensboro, North Carolina, to protest against segregation.

December: The US Supreme Court rules that it is unlawful to segregate travellers in interstate rail and bus stations.

1961 Mixed groups of African American and white people organize the Freedom Rides. They travel south by bus to challenge segregation in transport.

November: The Interstate Commerce Commission introduces new rules to stop segregation in transport facilities.

1963 Betty Friedan publishes *The Feminine Mystique*.

1964 The Labour Party wins the UK general election.

April: The Mississippi Freedom Democratic Party (MFDP) is established to challenge the all-white Democratic Party.

June onwards: The Mississippi Freedom Summer programme takes place to increase African American voter registration and challenge inequality.

July: Civil Rights Act is passed in the USA.

1965 Voting Rights Act is passed, allowing all US citizens to register to vote.

1966 The National Organization for Women (NOW) is founded.

1967 Barbara Castle introduces the breathalyser test in the UK.

1968 **April**: Martin Luther King Jr is assassinated.

June: Women workers at the Ford factory in Dagenham, London, go on strike for equal pay with male workers.

September: NOW protests at the Miss America contest in Atlantic City.

1969 Barbara Castle introduces the White Paper "In Place of Strife", which leads to conflict with the trade unions and fails to become law.

NOW organizes Public Accommodations Week to highlight discrimination against women in public places.

1970 **January:** The Equal Pay Act is passed in the UK.

August: NOW organizes women's marches across the USA.

1971 **July**: Betty Friedan and Bella Abzug co-found the National Women's Political Caucus (NWPC).

1972 The Equal Rights Amendment (ERA) passes in the US Senate, but eventually fails because not enough states pass it.

Find out more

Books

A 1960s Childhood: From Thunderbirds to Beatlemania, Paul Feeney (The History Press, 2010)

I Can Remember the 1960s, Sally Hewitt (Franklin Watts, 2010)

Websites

www.bbc.co.uk
Search for "clip 3515". This is a video titled "Greater freedom for women in the 1960s". It is about changes for women in Britain.

www.bbc.co.uk/radio4/womanshour/ timeline/1960.shtml
This website gives a timeline of significant events (1960–1969) that affected women.

www.cottontown.org/Politics/Blackburn% 20Members%20of%20Parliament/Pages/ Barbara-Castle.aspx#1

This website has a biography of Barbara Castle with photos.

www.uic.edu/orgs/cwluherstory/_notes/ GrrlSmarts/sawhney.html

This is a student's essay about the US women's movement.

Glossary

abortion medical operation to end a pregnancy at an early stage

civil rights rights that every person in a society has to be treated equally, for example to be able to vote or work, whatever their sex, race or religion

cooperative owned and run by the people involved, with the profits shared between them

couturier top fashion designer

discrimination practice of treating somebody or a particular group in society less fairly than others

feminist women's rights activist

freelance earning money by selling your work or services to several different organizations rather than being employed by one particular organization

grassroots ordinary people in society or in an organization, rather than the leaders or people who make decisions

opposition in politics, the main political party that is opposed to the government

personnel officer the person in a company who deals with employing and training people

resolution formal statement of an opinion agreed on by an organization, especially by means of a vote

segregation act or policy of separating people of different race, religion or sex and treating them in a different way

spin doctor person whose job is to present information to the public about a politician or an organization in the most positive way

stockings garment worn by women to cover the legs, held up by an elasticated strip at the top of the thigh

Index

112